P9-CNB-532

Let's Laugh a Little

Little Jokes With a BIG Message

Leroy Brownlow

To

_____

From

_____

Date

_____

Let's Laugh a Little

Let's Laugh a Little

Little Jokes With a BIG Message

Leroy Brownlow

Brownlow
Publishing Company, Inc.

Brownlow Gift Books

Foreword

This is a joke book clean enough to have in your home for your children, clean enough to take to church. But this volume is more than jokes. Each joke has a stated moral, a lesson. So in addition to humor, it is a book on the philosophies of life. The world loves a joke, and one that has both a laugh and a lesson is appreciated all the more. The humor gives entertainment and the lesson gives enlightenment.

Here we present humorous, illustrative material that will spice speeches for preachers, teachers, statesmen and all speakers; will tickle the funnybone for everybody in daily living; and will add zest and laughter to conversation in ordinary pastime.

Just having this book or a similar one in a home can lend credibility to one's reputation as a person of wit and humor. This is important because humor is such a warm, appealing, magnetic quality that no one wishes to admit that he lacks it. F. M. Colby said, "Men will confess to treason, murder, arson, false teeth, or a wig. How many of them will own up to a lack of humor?"

There is no magnetism or charm in a dismal, bland, insipid life. A corpse never smiles, but why be a corpse when one is still living?

Truly a little humor can do much for a person in many ways: It can break up the clouds and let the sun shine. Falling spirits are lifted by a walk through the Hall of

Humor. It can rescue a person from the doldrums which mar the spark and vibrancy of life. It is possible for one to laugh himself or herself into a new outlook. How constructive it is to spice life with unblemished fun that has no suggestion of roughhewn coarseness, or skewed sacrilege, or debasing irreverence. A good joke is a good relaxer. When the mind is relaxed the whole body responds. Actually, it is psychosomatic medicine that helps mentally and physically. This was stated by Solomon who said: "A merry heart doeth good like a medicine: but a broken spirit drieth the bones"—Proverbs 17:22.

It is noteworthy that Jesus effectively used humor in teaching. He spoke of "blind guides, which strain at a gnat and swallow a camel" (Matthew 23:24). Profound teaching in a comical setting. Likewise, He gave a lesson on pious hypocrisy and blind intolerance by asking, "And why beholdest thou the mote that is in thy brother's eye, but considereth not the beam that is in thine own eye?" (Matthew 7:3). This satire in which a man with a two by four sticking out his head proposes to extract a speck from his brother's eye is very humorous. Think what a cartoonist could do with these examples.

Now we present these jokes and their morals to the public with the hope that they may fill a special need in our society.

Leroy Brownlow

a young minister made his farewell speech before leaving to go as a missionary to an island known for its headhunters.

In his conclusion he said, "I am most grateful for your kind wishes, free generosity and sincere prayers. On that distant shore when I am surrounded by unsightly, cruel, curious savages, I shall always be reminded of you."

✦ **There are headhunters in distant lands and there are headhunters here at home; the difference is: here they perform the severance in a more sophisticated way.**

a man whose wife had been dead six months went to a psychic to get him to contact her. After awhile he was told to go ahead and speak.

He said, "Mary, how are you?"

"Just fine, just fine. I've never had such a pleasant time before," she replied.

"You mean you're enjoying yourself in heaven more than you enjoyed being with me on earth?"

She answered, "Well now, Henry, I'm not in heaven."

✦ **Some people can make earth so discordant that hell looks peaceful.**

9

a young man went into a college class with the letters BAIK across his tee shirt. The professor kept wondering what it meant. Finally, he stopped his lecture and asked, "Would you mind telling me what those letters on your shirt mean?"

The freshman replied, "BAIK—Boy, am I confused."

The professor smiled and said, "You don't spell confused with a 'K.'"

The student answered, "Now that just goes to show how really confused I am."

✦ **We don't have to announce our confusion— the word gets around.**

*T*here was a family that lived some ten miles from town. The land was rough and the family was rougher. They were members of the church but had been AWOL for a long time. The preacher had tried several times to edify them but his efforts were always impolitely spurned. However, when one of the boys was bitten by a rattlesnake the father sent another boy to fetch the minister.

The father, pale and excited, asked the preacher to pray. Whereupon, the preacher began: "Dear God, we thank Thee for rattlesnakes. We thank Thee that one has bitten Tom. We pray that Thou will send one to bite Carl. And we pray that Thou will send the biggest one of all to bite the old man, for only rattlesnakes will do this family any good."

✦ **What does it take for us to come to ourselves?**

a boy of 12 made this request of his father: "Dad, will you go to a private P.T.A. meeting with me tonight?"

"What do you mean? Private meeting?"

"Just you and I and the principal," answered the boy.

✦ **A crisis by any other name is still a crisis.**

a man woke up in the night slightly shaking. Thinking he was taking a cold, he got up and took some cold tablets and went back to bed. The next morning, feeling okay, he went out to get his newspaper which had this headline screaming at him: Earthquake Shakes City in Night.

✦ **We can jump to the wrong conclusion.**

a young man in a prominent family, a victim of alcohol, got lighted up in a town some thirty miles from home. He went to a telephone and called the funeral home in his hometown. Using a fictitious name, he told them that he was with the funeral home there and that they had the body of Bob Brown who was killed in a car accident; that they would embalm the body and transport it to the funeral home in the boy's town and that they should notify his parents.

The family lived about two miles from town with a lane running from the highway to their house.

The news flashed like lightning. It wasn't long until there was a big crowd of relatives and friends that filled the house and overflowed into a big yard.

The weeping parents sat in chairs beside each other in the living room. As they shook with grief they would sob out such statements as, "I hope the body isn't mangled. Oh, I hope he wasn't drunk when the end came. Nothing! Nothing! Nothing ever hit me so hard! I don't think I can stand it. Oh, if I just had him once again as a romping boy at my feet."

Never before on those premises had there been so much hugging and kissing and coffee drinking.

The crowd remained, though the midnight hour approached. Then suddenly a car turned off the highway and headed down the lane. They felt that surely news was coming to tell them that the body had been delivered to the funeral home. All anxiously awaited. Everything was exceedingly quiet.

Then that car came to a sudden halt in the yard, and that big old boy crawled out of it so drunk he could hardly walk. He took three or four staggering steps toward the crowd and said, "Well, folks, did you ever see a corpse walking?"

✦ Just believing something is true doesn't make it true.

little boy's first day at school was highlighted by his telling his teacher about his dog.

Teacher inquired: "What kind is he?"

"Oh, he's a mixed-up kind," replied the boy, "but more cocker scandal."

✦ **No matter how mixed-up a dog is,
he has purebred loyalty.**

boss rebuked his new secretary for revising his letters, telling her not to do that again, to take it the way he gives it.

"Now take this letter," he ordered.

Two days later Mr. Sid Sams received the following letter:

"Mr. J or J. M. or something—look it up. Sams—sounds like the plural of a given name. Dear Mr. Sams, hmmm, I need to say something straight to that Jerk. The last shipment of sugar wasn't a sweet deal, no good. Scratch that out. I want you to know that unless you can furnish us with quality sugar you can keep that cheap stuff. No, mark that out and put we won't be buying no more.

"Now read the letter over. No, don't do that. I've already wasted too much time on them bums. They ought to have to eat it all themselves, spoon by spoon."

✦ **Sometimes we don't really want what we ask for.**

a country preacher called on a farm family about lunch time. They were short on food; but, being long on hospitality, they asked him to eat with them. Then they asked him to express thanks. He looked over the prospects and all he saw was a bowl of cooked beets. This was his prayer: "Dear Lord, we thank Thee for that which beats all."

✦ **Blessed is the person who can adjust himself to what he has and look upon it as that which beats all.**

a few years ago, according to a national magazine, the Internal Revenue Service received $400.00 from an unnamed person with the note: "I owe you a lot of money. My conscience has been bothering me so much that I can't sleep. Here is $400.00. If I still can't sleep, I'll send you some more later."

✦ **Conscience can become a tormentor for all of us— unless it has become seared.**

While a hunter was in the forest he took aim at a bear. The bear said, "Hold on, let's negotiate and see if we can't get this problem worked out."

The hunter said, "Okay."

The bear continued, "What do you want?"

The hunter replied, "I want a fur coat."

The bear said, "I want a full stomach."

They worked it out. The bear got a full stomach and the hunter got a fur coat.

✦ **Beware of some negotiations lest you end up with a fur coat.**

a coward stated that he was cut out to be brave but was sewed up wrong. "My spine extends down to my feet, and now when danger lurks I take off running."

✦ **One of the soul's highest accomplishments is courage.**

*I*n leaving church one Sunday, a member commented: "We had a good time at church today. If the Lord had been there, that would have made it perfect."

✦ **Anything that keeps the Lord from attending a church is enough to keep the rest of us from going.**

a speaker at a public gathering heard someone hiss. Cold silence followed.

Finally the speaker said, "There are two things that hiss—a snake and a fool. Stand up and be identified."

✦ **Courtesy requires us to let a speaker have his say, though we disagree with him.**

*I*n the winter when night came early a funeral was concluded at the cemetery. The family left and the attendants got ready to lower the casket. Lo and behold, the grave was too short which necessitated that they lengthen it. The sun had already set. Night was rapidly approaching. As a worker in the grave was digging, the director said, "We're going to have to hurry; it will soon be dark."

The laborer abruptly stopped, straightened up, and said, "Let me tell you something: if we're not through when dark comes I'm leaving."

"Why? The dead won't hurt you."

"That's not what I'm afraid of; I'm afraid I might hurt myself," answered the workman.

✦ **Our biggest threat is ourselves.**

A preacher's son was asked if his daddy ever preached a sermon more than once.

"Yes, but it doesn't sound the same."

"How's that?"

"He just hollers in a different place," replied the boy.

✦ **Changing the delivery doesn't change the substance.**

a boy refused to take a bath. His mother insisted. Still he objected. She asked, "Why do you think you shouldn't?"

He replied, "My Sunday School teacher said that we shouldn't do anything in private that we wouldn't do in public."

✦ **Let's keep a distinction between what should be private and what should be public.**

a speaker at a political rally thought he heard his opponent in the front row say something. So he suddenly stopped and asked, "What did you say?"

"Nothing," was the reply.

"Yes, of course, but how did you express it this time?" replied the speaker.

✦ **Let's do more than talk—say something.**

T wo friends were discussing the brilliance of a third party.

"How smart is he? Is he as smart as you are?" inquired one of them.

"No, I guess he's about like you are," was the answer.

✦ **Some of our own answers show that we're not as smart as we think we are.**

a preacher was dictating his sermon to his secretary. But every few words he would say, "Scratch that out, and start all over."

"Is the Lord telling you what to say?" inquired the secretary.

"Yes, of course, He is," replied the minister.

"Then in that case I wish the Lord would make up His mind what He wants to say," responded the woman.

✦ God shouldn't have to take the rap for man's mistakes.

a young lawyer was asked to speak to a large civic club. He had worked hard on his message, hoping to make a hit. But when he got up to address them his speech left him. He coughed, pulled out his handkerchief, coughed again, looked to the left, looked to the right, looked to the ceiling, coughed again, and said, "I have a very good address. It is 415 Walnut Street, and I'm going there now." And he walked out.

✦ A short speech can be remembered.

a second grade teacher in a rural school asked Paul the question: "If you had eight chickens and a thief stole three of them, how many would you have left?"

He replied, "I would say eight."

"Why would you say eight?"

"Because my daddy would shoot that chicken thief before he could get out of the yard."

✦ **What some don't see, others do.**

*a*s a visitor was leaving a church service, the minister asked him if he had any suggestions for improvement.

Having observed the untidiness of the place, he said, "Yes, I think you need some sweeping reforms."

✦ **Some sweeping reforms go way beyond a broom or a vacuum cleaner.**

a hunter was hunting in a region known for its lakes—and mosquitoes. The latter were eating him up, leaving itching welts all over the exposed portions of his body.

Finally, in desperation, he prayed: "Dear Lord, deliver me from my enemies, these flying blood suckers; I'll take care of the bears myself."

✦ **There are times when we think it's easier to handle the big problems than the little ones.**

a construction foreman said to a worker on the job, "I'd like to know something: Why is it that the other workers carry four or five boards at a time while you carry only one?"

"I suppose, sir," replied the worker, "that they are too lazy to go back and get another board."

✦ **If you make yourself a lightweight, you are not prepared for heavy burdens.**

*O*n Sunday morning the preacher spoke very tenderly on *The Compassionate Jesus*, emphasizing that Jesus loved little children. The following week he was in a different role; he was director of the congregation's Vacation Bible School. After a few days his nerves became tattered. An extra pressure was the contractor pouring concrete on the parking lot. Then the breaking point came. He saw Tommy walking in the concrete, and yelled, "Tommy! Tommy! Tommy! Get out of there! Don't you know better than that?"

Tommy, mother's little darling who had never before been rebuked, went home crying.

Immediately the angry mother called the nerve-tattered minister and reminded him of last Sunday's sermon. "It was beautiful and sweet rhetoric," she said, "but what about the practice? If you love Tommy, why were you so mean and harsh to him?"

"Hear me, lady," replied the preacher, "I do love Tommy, but I must admit I love him in the abstract—not in the concrete."

✦ **The best of people can be vexed.**

*I*n discussing a miserly tightwad in the town one lady said, "I noticed that he's getting awfully deaf."

Her neighbor responded, "No, he's not getting deaf; he can hear a dollar bill light in the snow."

✦ **When money is involved, the hearing can improve.**

a lady just out of college applied as a proofreader for a newspaper.

The editor queried her: "Do you understand the momentous responsibility of this position?"

"Yes, I think so," responded the applicant. "Each time you make a mistake in the paper just blame it on me, and I'll never say a word or tell anybody."

✦ **No one should expect others to bear his own mistakes.**

a minister and his seven-year-old son were out driving. As they passed a horse racetrack the boy was held in wonderment. He exclaimed, "Look, Daddy, look. All the pews are filled."

✦ **People gravitate toward their greatest interest.**

a preacher got off a plane and walked into the terminal building. He said to a little boy he met, "Son, do the people in this town enjoy their religion?"

"Them that's got it do," was the lightning response.

✦ **Pretended religion brings no real joy.**

*T*wo men were out on the lake fishing on morning. About 10:00 a.m. one fisherman sa we ought to be ashamed of ourselves. It is now church time and here we are on the lake."

The other one responded, "I couldn't have gone anyway; my wife is sick."

✦ **Excuses come easily when the mind is inclined.**

*T*he preacher called on an elderly woman who had been missing church and admonished her that she should be thinking about the hereafter.

She told him: "I do all the time. No matter where I am: in the living room, the kitchen, upstairs, downstairs, or the basement, I ask myself, 'What am I here after?'"

✦ **The time comes when a person swaps one here after for another hereafter.**

*I*t was observed that a bachelor especially enjoyed visiting his brother and holding his brother's little girl on his lap. His explanation was: "This allows me to have a girl on my knees without having her on my hands."

✦ **Marriage demands responsibility.**

a worker in a plant bought a new small car known for good gasoline mileage. Other workers for two or three weeks would slip out and put some gasoline in it. They had the most amusing time glancing and winking at each other, as he would tell that he had a car that would give 70 miles per gallon.

✦ **Anything too good needs to be looked into.**

a tightwad who was drowning in a lake was pulled to shore by a stranger.

The miser's wife suggested that he give the rescuer $100.00 for saving his life.

The skinflint argued, "Maybe I should give him only $50.00, because I was only half dead when he saved me."

✦ **The love of money causes us to underestimate the value of life.**

a man who was blaming the world's woes on education said to the preacher, "I know I'm ignorant; I'm glad I'm ignorant; I just hope I get ignoranter."

The preacher placed his hand on the man's shoulder and said, "Brother, I feel sure that God will grant your request."

✦ **None can be so ignorant as he who delights in ignorance.**

a church member, extremely proud of the preacher, inadvertently spoke more than he intended. He said, "We have the best preacher that money can buy."

✦ **In the ministry no man should be for sale.**

a teacher stated to Raymond: "Listen to me—this is the fifth time this week I've had to punish you. What do you have to say?"

"I'm glad it's Friday," replied Raymond.

✦ **Changing behavior is more important than changing days.**

a swimmer who had a rash called on the preacher for help. He said, "I thought maybe you know what Jesus did when he cured the sick of 'divers diseases.'"

✦ **Where there's an itch, there's apt to be a scratch.**

a young man from the country took a job in a store in a little town. He had a hat with his name stamped on the inside band, which he would leave in a room during store hours. Other workers bought another hat exactly like his with his name in it, except it was one size larger. They exchanged the hats. When the new worker put it on, it came down to his ears. He pulled it off, thinking it wasn't his, but there was his name in it. So he folded some paper and lined the band.

The next day the pranksters put the paper lining in the original hat and left it in exchange. Then the next time the worker put on his hat it was way too small, stood on his head. He removed the lining and it fit exactly. This game was played two or three days. He knew it was his hat—that wasn't the problem. So he decided that he was the problem—that he was going wacky.

✦ **The person who has a problem is not always the problem.**

Some grown boys at the village store would hold before a ten-year-old boy a quarter and a dime, and ask him which one he wanted. He would always take the dime. Then they would laugh and poke fun at his inability.

One day an older man called the boy aside and said, "They're making sport of you. Don't you know the quarter is worth more than the dime?"

"Yes, I know," replied the boy, "but if I take the quarter they'll quit doing it."

✦ **When you think you're making a fool of the other fellow, he might be making a fool out of you.**

"Oh, preacher, I wish I could take my gold with me," stated a dying man.

"It might melt," was the consoling reply.

✦ **He who wishes to take his gold into the next world is not prepared to go.**

There was a dry cleaning business that put up a catchy sign: "We have worked on the same spot for 12 years."

✦ **Try and try again—and keep trying.**

drunk was wandering through a cemetery. With blurry eyes he read the epitaphs. One said, "Not dead, but sleeping."

He squinted and said, "Listen, Bud, you ain't fooling nobody but yourself."

✦ **Why should we think it is harder for the Creator to give life the second time than it was the first time?**

*A*fter a beloved dentist in a little town died, his friends wanted to do something special in memory of him. So they erected a large tombstone inscribed with an epitaph that emphasized his life's work: "He is now filling his last cavity."

✦ **From the cradle to the grave, one generation follows another.**

*F*amily and friends went to hear a young man just out of theological school who claimed that he had been called to preach. One of his hearers later commented: "It must have been a local call—not long distance."

✦ **No matter what the calling is, in the last analysis, the public decides if we can or can't.**

a salesman who was out of state making his calls picked up his hometown paper and read to his surprise that he was dead. He pinched himself to be sure he was alive and called the paper. He stated, "You ran an item in your paper yesterday that I'm dead."

"Yes, we sure did, and from where are you calling?" was the pointed answer.

✦ **Some questions can be very shocking.**

a minister at the conclusion of his lesson in a class of middle-aged couples recognized the visitors. He looked at one lady in the second row and said, "What's your name, please?"

She very indignantly said, "What? You mean you don't remember me? You were at my house just last week."

The minister replied, "Lady, with no offense, let me tell you how it is: I have to get acquainted with all you women twice—how you look at home and how you look in public."

✦ **Sometimes an effort to put another person on the spot boomerangs.**

A very agitated citizen at a political rally confronted a politician with these biting words: "You slicker, I wouldn't vote for you if you were Jesus Christ."

He quickly retorted, "If I were Jesus Christ, you couldn't vote for me—you wouldn't be in my precinct."

✦ **When we sling mud, we need to get ready to eat dirt.**

A man who was mighty ill asked his wife to send for the minister of a certain denomination.

She asked, "Harry, why don't you send for your own preacher?"

He replied, "Oh, no, no, I wouldn't dare expose my preacher to this disease I have."

✦ **Our concern for others should be for all others.**

A United States Senator made a highly publicized speech on "Great Senators."

When a person who heard the message was asked by another person who didn't hear it what he thought about it, he replied, "I'm sure there's one less than he thinks."

✦ **If we could buy some people at their true value and sell them at their self-appraised value, we could get rich on one trade.**

*W*hen little Johnny returned home from church, his mother, who didn't bother to go asked him, "Did you behave in church this morning?"

"I sure did," answered Johnny. "I heard a woman behind me say, 'I never before in all my life saw a child behave like that.'"

✦ **As the bush is bent so leans the tree.**

*I*n the midst of a preaching service attended by a thousand people, a woman stood up and said, "I would like to ask a question."

The minister replied, "Lady, the Bible says that if a woman wants to know anything, let her ask her husband at home. But—your husband being who he is—go ahead."

The laughter shook the building.

✦ **Be sure we ask questions for answers and not for recognition.**

Two fellows who had run out of water while crossing a desert began discussing how thirsty they were.

One said that he was so thirsty he could drink a barrel of water.

The other one stated, "I'm thirstier than that—I'm as thirsty as a child who has just gone to bed."

✦ **Thirst for assurance can be greater than thirst for water.**

*W*hen a man appeared on the job his boss asked, "What happened to your ears?"

"While I was cooking, the phone rang and I picked up the egg beater instead of the phone."

"But what happened to the other ear?"

"That guy called back," was the forlorn answer.

✦ **If we don't learn the lesson the first time, we are bound to repeat it.**

*I*n some families Sunday dinner always consists of Roasted Preacher. In one family as they sat at the dinner table they were very profuse in criticizing the preacher's sermon. They really chewed him out.

But it was little John who took the cake. Finally he said, "I didn't think it was so bad. What do you expect for a quarter?"

✦ **It is easy to criticize something in which we have so little invested.**

*T*here was a tightfisted owner of a motel who had this sign underneath the big clock in the lobby: "For use of guests only."

✦ **There are some who won't give you the time of day.**

a boy handed a plate of two cookies—one large, one small—to another boy to take one. He took the large cookie.

"You selfish thing. I thought if I let you make the choice, you would pick the small one and leave the large one for me," stated the scheming lad.

✦ **An unselfish gesture may actually be a selfish one.**

a man called on a minister who promptly asked, "Are you seeking salvation?"

"No," replied the man, "I'm a bus driver and I came to see if you would tell me how you get everybody to the rear of the building."

✦ **The front seats are always taken first—except at church.**

a school board had a meeting with the principal because an irate mother had complained.

A trustee said, "You should handle matters judiciously. You should stroke the fur the right way."

"Sir, I did stroke the fur the right way," stated the principal, "but the cat was going the wrong direction."

✦ **It's so much easier to walk in peace if we're going the same direction.**

a minister's wife enjoyed collecting antiques. One Sunday a friend of hers, as she entered the foyer, handed the preacher a rolling pin and stated, "When you see your wife, let her have it."

✦ **Words can be construed in keeping with the ears of the listener.**

a man was leading prayer at the evening hour at church. During the prayer the lights went out. When the prayer was concluded he opened his eyes and there was pitch-black darkness. He cried out, "Oh Lord, I've been struck blind."

✦ **Every person in darkness is blind.**

T wo little boys were talking about going to heaven. One said, "I know I'm going to heaven, 'cause I've got it all figured out. I'm going up to the door and I'm gonna go in and out, and in and out. Then finally someone will say, 'Get in or get out, but shut that door.' Then I'm gonna scoot inside and shut the door behind me."

✦ **The only way to go to heaven is to let the Lord give the directions.**

a n English professor asked a student to remain after class. He pointed out that the student would have to do some dramatic climbing to pass.

"What shall I have to do to get up there?" inquired the student.

"You need to get aboard a flying Chaucer," replied the educator.

✦ **Books can lift us into the clouds— but only if we get into them.**

*T*wo little boys were competitors in the lemonade business. Their stands were across the street from each other. One sold his for 25¢ a glass, the other for 20¢ a glass.

A woman stopped at the 25¢ stand and asked, "Why do you sell yours for 25¢ and the boy across the street sells his for 20¢?"

"Because the cat didn't fall into mine," replied the wheeler-dealer. (Neither did the cat fall into the other one's vessel.)

✦ **A person can tell the truth and at the same time imply an untruth.**

A man went to see a doctor to whom he said: "I feel all right at night, but during the day I take a headache, my eyes bulge and I get dizzy."

After the examination the doctor said, "I can't pinpoint the cause of your ailment, something mysterious, but with your symptoms it would have to be very serious."

"How serious, doctor? Give it to me straight."

"I would say you have about six months," replied the doctor.

The patient accepted the devastating news realistically: decided to buy some new clothes, go and spend, and crowd a lifetime of living into six months.

In buying some new shirts he asked for size 15 1/2. However, the clerk measured his neck and said, "You need size 16 1/2."

The patient argued, "No, I know what size I wear. I want 15 1/2."

The clerk replied, "Okay, I can give you 15 1/2. But I'm telling you one thing for sure: if you wear 15 1/2, your head will start hurting, your eyes will bulge and you will get dizzy."

✦ **Most of our ailments are not as bad as we think.**

*T*he college counselor asked the young man what was bothering him.

"The girl I think I'm in love with has refused to date me," explained the boy.

"Don't let that stop you," said the counselor. "Oftentimes when a woman says 'No,' she really means 'Yes.'"

"But, she didn't say 'No.' She made a face, stuck out her tongue and said, 'Do you think I'm crazy?'"

✦ **There's a way to say No, and there's a way to really say *No*.**

*A*fter the service was completed at the cemetery the man's widow got in the big funeral car as the lone rider—no other relatives.

On the way home the driver said, "Sarah, I don't want you to be offended. This is a compliment. I have been in love with you for years, but I wouldn't say anything about it because I didn't want to come between a man and his wife. I have always been a minute late and a foot short. I don't want that to happen again. Your husband is gone. So if you should ever decide to get married again, just remember I asked you first."

"Thank you, Tom, but the doctor has already asked me," was the heartbreaking reply.

✦ **Coming up late and short makes a difference in what you get.**

a preacher who had spent hours studiously writing the notes for his Sunday sermon forgot and left them at home. He began his sermon: "Since I have forgotten my notes, I am forced to rely on the Lord for help. Next Sunday I shall come better prepared."

✦ **Incongruous words can make a mockery of our profession.**

a little girl asked an old preacher who was visiting them: "Were you in the ark?"

"Oh, no, no," answered the preacher.

"Then why didn't you drown?" inquired the little girl.

✦ **A little child shall ask what everyone else is thinking.**

*W*hile the custodian was laying some carpet on the platform in the church auditorium he unintentionally scattered some tacks on the floor.

"Look here, James," said the minister, "what do you think would happen if I stepped on one of those tacks in the middle of a sermon?"

"Well, I'm not a learned man," replied the custodian, "but I reckon there'd be one point you wouldn't linger on."

✦ **When we make a point, we don't have to camp out on it.**

a couple went out one night and left their baby in the care of a baby sitter. When they returned they anxiously asked, "How did things go?"

The sitter replied, "About ten minutes ago the baby swallowed a bug, but you have nothing to worry about—I fed him some insect powder."

✦ **The cure can be worse than the ailment.**

a fisherman was talking about his latest fishing trip. He said, "I caught a fish that weighed seven pounds, but it got away."

"But how do you know it weighed seven pounds, if it got away?" inquired a listener.

The fisherman thought for a moment and said, "Because it had scales on it."

✦ **Quick wit can even save a fish story.**

*W*e get the impression that when some people confess their sins they're not confessing—just bragging.

✦ **When there's glory in sin there's something wrong with society's standard.**

a little boy told a lie. The father—wanting to break him from lying—said, "Let me tell you what will happen if you tell lies. A mean old man with a tail and horns like a cow and fingers a foot long with nails that stick out another six inches will come and get you. He will take you to a faraway forest and make you work day and night with nothing to eat but bread and water. You don't want to tell another lie, do you?"

The boy replied, "No, because you can tell them much bigger than I can."

✦ **Never let your children see in you what you dislike in them.**

a young preacher heard an older preacher say in a sermon, "The happiest days of my life were spent in the arms of another man's wife—my mother."

Thinking it was cute, he decided to include it in his next sermon. He said, "The happiest days of my life were spent in the arms of another man's wife." Then his memory went blank, he coughed, swallowed and started over: "The happiest days of my life were spent in the arms of another man's wife." Still not able to remember, he blushed and said, "To save my life, I can't remember who she was."

✦ **A failing memory can be embarrassing.**

a young lover dipped his pen in romanticism and wrote these precious words to his sweetheart: "The moon shines on a lonely man tonight because you are there and I am here. The pain gnaws at a restless heart. The feeling I have for you defies the pen of any writer to describe, and would render speechless the tongue of any orator who would attempt to expound it. This love reaches beyond all human limitations. I would be willing to crawl through a pit of snakes just to look upon that lovely face of yours. I would be willing to climb the highest mountain peak just to see the gleam in those ocean-blue eyes nature has endowed you with. I would swim the highest swollen river just to be by your side." He signed it, "Lovingly and devotedly yours, Henry."

Then at the bottom he added this postscript, "I'll see you Wednesday night if it doesn't rain."

✦ **Hypocrisy is easily detected though it comes clothed in beautiful garb.**

a policeman stopped a driver who had just run a stop sign.

"Now don't tell me, lady, that you didn't see that stop sign," commented the officer.

"Oh, yes, Mr. Policeman, I saw the sign—I just didn't see you," replied the woman.

✦ Policemen are stronger deterrents to traffic violations than traffic signs.

a man who lost his wife in death had a double marker erected with these tender and expressive words inscribed: "My light has gone out." At that time he thought he would never want to get married again. However, after a couple of years he began to think of marriage. But every time he thought of it he was haunted by that inscription on the tombstone. Greatly disturbed, he finally went to a counselor and explained that he would like to get married again but was having trouble with the double marker and the inscription: "My light has gone out."

The adviser suggested: "Just inscribe this statement on it—'I have struck another match.'"

✦ **The living should not be buried with the dead— the world must keep turning, and the living must keep living.**

a farmer had the misfortune of having a cow run over by a train. Later he had a stranger come and ask about buying a cow: He wanted to know how much a cow was worth.

The farmer replied, "Well, that depends on whether you are a claim agent for the railroad or the tax assessor for the county."

✦ **Walking in the straight way leaves no room for double dealings.**

a church in a rural area made a special drive to raise money. One farmer stated that he had a calf and when it grew up he would sell it and give the money to the church. Months passed and they heard no more from him.

One Sunday when he drove on the church grounds the congregation was singing the old hymn, "The Half Has Not Yet Been Told." Thinking they were singing, "The calf has not yet been sold," he became angry, turned around, went home and hasn't been back.

✦ **Our own conscience can hear things that were never said.**

O ne man asked another one: "What would you say are the chief problems in the world today?"

"I don't know and I don't care," was his answer.

The inquirer responded: "You have just named both of them: 'I don't know'—ignorance; and 'I don't care'—indifference."

✦ **Each person has the responsibility to make the world a better place than he found it.**

a Sunday School teacher asked the question, "Who led the children of Israel out of Egypt?" and at the same time looked directly at a boy.

"I didn't do it," he said. "We just moved here from Houston."

✦ **Children can come up with some shocking justifications.**

*a*t a revival the preacher stated, "All who want to go to heaven stand up." All stood up except a drunk. Seeing him, the preacher then said, "All who want to go to hell stand up." The drunk wobbled to his feet. The preacher said, "You mean you want to go to hell?"

The poor rummy said, "N-no, I-I really don't, but I thought you looked so lonesome standing there by yourself."

✦ **Be sure you know for what and with whom you stand.**

a preacher who went several minutes over his usual time in a sermon apologized at the last. A good sister who wanted to comfort him later said, "Brother, you didn't preach a long time; it just seemed like a long time."

✦ **Deliver us from some comforters.**

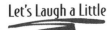 ram on the ranch committed suicide. The reason: The rancher drove up in a pickup playing, "There Will Never Be Another You."

+ **Before taking drastic steps it is best to check our information one more time.**

A man who planned a vacation in Colorado hardly knew what to do with his dog. So he wrote the motel and asked if he could bring a dog. The motel manager wrote back:

"For 25 years I've been in this business. Never has a dog been careless with a cigarette and set fire to the bed. Never have I found a motel towel or blanket in a dog's suitcase. Nor have I ever found a whiskey ring on a dresser caused by a dog's leaving a bottle on it. Furthermore, never have I called the police to evict a disorderly dog. We welcome the dog and if he will vouch for you, you may come along with him."

+ **Dogs are easier to care for than some people.**

*T*he alcoholic attempted to justify his topsy lifestyle on the ground that the Bible says, "Use a little wine for thy stomach's sake."

But his wife reasoned: "It says, 'Use a little wine for thy stomach's sake,' but I didn't know your stomach ached."

✦ **It's easy for one to justify in his own mind what he's bent on doing.**

*Y*ears ago in the villages a boy would take his date to the door of the church where she would go in and sit down, but he would stay outside and chew and whittle with the other fellows.

A young man was warned by his girl's father to get her home by a certain time. As the preacher preached on and on, the boy became nervous. Finally, he decided to go in and get her. As he appeared inside, the preacher said, "Young man, are you seeking salvation?"

He replied, "No, I'm seeking Sal Johnson. Is she here?"

✦ **Seek and ye shall find.**

*T*here are couples who clearly remember when and where they got married, but can't remember why.

✦ **The best marriage is one in which each considers the other better than himself or herself.**

a husband and wife who were having marital problems went to a psychologist. After awhile the professional got up from his chair and went over to the woman and hugged and hugged her very intensely. Then he turned to the husband and said, "This ought to be done every day."

The husband replied, "Doctor, I'm sorry but I can bring her only on Tuesday and Thursday."

✦ **Sometimes we fail to see that we are the answer.**

I n an open air revival the preacher had a question box for the people to drop in their unsigned questions. Each night he answered them before his sermon. One night he had this question: "Will you explain the difference between a preacher and a fool?" The audience chuckled, and after it subsided he read it again and everything got very quiet. Then he said, "If the person who wrote this question will come up here and stand beside me, I think the audience can see the difference." The crowd went wild with laughter.

✦ **Fools have a way of revealing themselves.**

wo families went to the mountains on vacation where they shared a lodge in the forest. One of the men went walking among the trees where he attracted the attention of a bear which chased him. As he ran—the bear after him—he yelled, "Open the door." As he ran through the house and out the back door, he hollered, "You skin him and I'll go get another one."

✦ **How many times we dump our problems on others while we run out the back door.**

a husband stated that his wife was having an exercise problem.

"What kind of exercise is she taking?" asked the friend.

"She's piling up bills and jumping at conclusions," replied the worried man.

✦ **Unless the exercise is suitable it should not be taken.**

a baker who was about to go broke went to see a financial consultant.

After an analysis, he said, "The trouble is you're not mixing enough hard work with the yeast to raise the dough."

✦ **This is a work-a-world — must work to have.**

a bachelor was asked, "Why is it that you never married?"

"Well, this is why," he replied, "I kept looking for the perfect woman."

"And you never found her?"

"Oh, yes, but my luck being the way it is—she was looking for the perfect man."

✦ **Don't expect more from others than you're willing to give.**

a young wife stated, "We've been married a whole year and have never quarreled."

"What do you do when there's a difference of opinion?" inquired the friend.

"In that case, and I'm right, my husband gives in."

"And what happens when he's right?"

"That has never happened," was her reply.

✦ **No person can be right all the time.**

a Sunday School teacher invited the parents of her students to visit her class. Wanting to show them off and make the parents proud, she asked them to pray the prayer they had prayed the night before.

One little girl prayed: "Dear Lord, don't give my parents any more children, because they don't know how to treat the one they've got."

✦ **We can depend on a child to make us think.**

t was Benjamin Franklin who said:

"Early to bed and early to rise,

Makes a man healthy, wealthy and wise."

A new version is:

"Late to bed and early to rise,

Makes a man baggy beneath the eyes."

✦ **We can't cheat on nature for long.**

When the dynamic evangelist asked his audience to stand if they wanted to go to heaven, all stood but the town drunk. Not wanting to be outdone, the preacher asked, "Don't you want to go to heaven?"

"Yes, but I thought you were trying to get up a load for tonight," replied the drunk, which brought down the house.

✦ **Timing is very important in everything.**

*T*here is the story of a hen and a pig that left the farm and went into town. Walking down the street, they saw the sign: Ham and Eggs.

The pig said, "Look there; for you that's just a contribution; but for me that's total commitment."

✦ **What the world needs—whether it is church, business or education—is total commitment.**

*O*ne man at church always prayed the same prayer—so much the same that everyone could go three words ahead of him. A portion of it went, "Oh Lord, since we last called upon Thee, the cobwebs have come between us and Thee. We pray that Thou will remove the cobwebs that we may once again look upon Thy face."

One Sunday, just as he got to the phrase "remove the cobwebs" another brother spoke a little louder than he intended, "Oh Lord, kill the spider!"

✦ **It is better to eliminate the cause than to remove the effect.**

a man who went from a poor condition to a rich condition in his old age knew he didn't have much time for luxurious living; so he decided to make a splash and go all-out in his funeral. His will specified that he be buried in a new pink Cadillac, sitting behind the wheel, dressed in a thousand dollar suit, with a cigar in his mouth, and with the radio playing, "Open That Pearly Gate."

Upon his death, every detail was carried out. As the crane operator was lowering that fancy Cadillac into that massive grave, he was overheard to say, "Now that's real living."

✦ **Real living is found in more than the finery that surrounds us in either life or death.**

*D*uring a long church service in which a man went to sleep, the preacher said, "John, wake up Harry; he's gone to sleep."

John replied, "You wake him up; you put him to sleep."

✦ **One's responsibility can't be shoved off on another.**

a father in a little town was so proud of his son who had moved to a big city for bigger opportunities. The exultant father stated that the boy had his feet on the ground, was doing well, that he had 5,000 people under him in his work.

A friend inquired, "What does he do?"

"Mows the grass in the cemetery," answered the father.

✦ **Any honorable job that is done well is a credit to the doer.**

a man who became very rich in the oil business gave some nice gifts to members of his family. He gave a $20,000.00 coat to his sister. To his brother he gave a $20,000.00 car. And to his mother he gave a $25,000.00 parrot that could speak five languages. Later he asked them how they liked their presents. These are the answers:

The sister said, "That's the most luxurious coat I ever saw. When I put it on the whole world lights up."

The brother answered: "It's a dream car. I never thought I would ever have anything like it. I'm the envy of my friends."

The mother responded: "A wonderful gift. Never before have I eaten such delicious fowl."

✦ **We need a true sense of values.**

I n discussing how much the late Harry was missed, a saddened friend said, "Harry was a real buddy, a true friend. And now it bothers me that I never did tell him how much I thought of him. When I get to heaven I'm going to tell him how much I appreciated him."

"What if he's not there?" inquired the other man.

"Well, in that case, I'll let you tell him for me," was the answer.

✦ **We're all going somewhere.**

a would-be author sent a manuscript to a publisher. An editor noticed that it had no punctuation marks. However, at the end there was a note that stated, "I'm no good at punctuation, so I'm enclosing a page of periods, commas, semicolons, colons, apostrophes, quotation marks, question marks and exclamation points. You can place them where they belong."

✦ **To get the job done right, we can't overlook the details.**

a father had always expressed opposition to his daughter's marrying a preacher. The daughter was insistent that her daddy go hear the young preacher she expected to marry. After hearing him, the father said, "I withdraw my opposition—what little preaching he does won't make any difference anyway."

✦ **At first we may not look like much, but God isn't through with us yet.**

I n a Sunday School class the teacher asked, "After creating Adam, why did God create Eve?"

A little girl replied, "I suppose that after looking at Adam, God said, 'I think I can do better the second time.'"

✦ **What God does defies human conclusions.**

a transient who had no identification papers dropped dead in a little town. For days the authorities and the funeral home labored to identify him and to notify his kin.

One day a man looked at him and said, "That's my brother; haven't seen him for years, but that's my brother. Get him out of that box, clothe him with a fine suit, and put him in an expensive casket. I shall be back this afternoon to see him again."

This thrilled the funeral director, for a liability had become an asset.

When the man who was paying the bill went back he saw that the mouth of the corpse had come slightly open; so he said, "This is not my brother. No. No. My brother didn't have teeth like that. This is not my brother. I'm not going to pay for it." And he walked out.

The disappointed director had a problem. He took the corpse out of the expensive casket and high-priced clothes, dressed him in cheap garb and put him in a beggarly coffin which was too short for him. Being too short, when the director pushed the man's feet down his head raised up. Then he went to the head and pushed it down and the man's feet lifted up. Back and forth he went three or four times, but he couldn't get both in at the same time.

Finally, he pushed his hand into the man's chest and said, "If you had kept your mouth shut, you would have gotten a decent burial."

✦ **An open mouth can close the door of opportunity.**

a motorist in a little town that had stores along the street noticed that a car had stopped. Thinking the car had stalled, he eased up behind it and began to push it. The woman behind the wheel became frantic, began blowing the horn and waving her hands. Out dashed a frenzied woman from a store, yelling, "What are you doing?"

The eager helper replied, "I'm giving her a push to start her car."

"She doesn't want a push," exclaimed the lady, "she just stopped so I could run in and get her some aspirins. Now we'll both need them."

✦ **Jumping at wrong conclusions lands us in trouble.**

a father said to his 12-year-old son, "Go get some wood and put it on the fire." The boy just sat there—listless. After a while the father repeated the order. Again the boy paid him no attention. A little later the father made the request for the third time. Nothing happened. Then after another four or five minutes the father said, "Son, don't you go and get any wood. There's one thing sure—you're going to mind me."

✦ **If the only way we can change a lawless society is to have no laws, then nobody is safe.**

a father and a son got into an argument that became extremely nasty. At the height of the bitterness the father yelled, "I'll tell you one thing—my father is better than yours."

✦ **Anger loosens the tongue and causes us to say things we don't even believe.**

a preacher preached a strong, powerful, emotional sermon on hell. At the conclusion he said, "We shall now stand and Deacon Jones will lead us in the song, 'Tell Mother I'll Be There.'"

✦ **Even good words at the wrong time are hurtful.**

a judge, thinking the pending case would not last long, agreed to meet his wife downtown at eleven o'clock. But he was mistaken. While the case was dragging, he nervously looked at his watch from time to time. Then unexpectedly the two opposing attorneys asked for another hour each to argue the case.

The judge said, "Request granted. But I promised to meet my wife downtown at eleven o'clock, so I shall be going. But when you get through you may look in this drawer and get my verdict. I wrote it out last night before I went to bed."

✦ **Fair-mindedness will not permit preconceived ideas.**

wo children argued as to which is more important: the sun or the moon. One of them contended that the moon is; because it shines at night when we need the light, while the sun shines in the daytime when we don't need it.

✦ **Sometimes we forget what makes the moon shine—and what makes us shine.**

uring a fire in a saloon, their parrot flew out the door and down the street where he entered an open window in a church. When the audience assembled on Sunday the parrot flew around in the auditorium three or four times, landed on the podium and squawked, "The building is different, but it's the same old crowd."

✦ **Our crowd of friends and conduct sooner or later reveal our character.**

farmer stated that he was going to enter his mule in the Kentucky Derby.

A friend said, "Surely, you don't think he has a chance to win."

"No," replied the farmer, "but I thought the association might do him good."

✦ **Wholesome associations encourage excellent morals, but evil associations corrupt them.**

66

a man who came into possession of a large fortune began pursuing a lifelong dream—to own a first-class racehorse. The manager of a horse ranch showed him an older one and commented, "This horse has won several races through the years." Then he paraded a colt before him and assured him, "This colt will become a famous racer like the other one."

The would-be buyer shook his head and stated, "You showed me a 'has-beener' and a 'goner-be,' but I'm looking for an 'isser.'"

✦ **The world is looking for an "isser."**

a young lady concluded her prayer with a simple unpretending request: "Dear Lord, I'm not asking for myself, but please, Lord, it would help a lot if you would send my mother a son-in-law."

✦ **Prayer is an opportunity for heart-searching and free expression.**

a seven-year-old girl went to see the president of a bank and asked him to make a contribution to their Girls Club.

The banker, wanting to test the girl, laid a dime and a dollar bill on the desk and said, "Take your choice."

She picked up the dime and said, "My mother has taught me that it's good manners to take the smallest piece." But she added as she picked up the dollar bill: "So I won't lose this dime, I'll take this piece of paper to wrap it up in."

✦ **There is money in thinking.**

A minister went to visit an old man who was known for his religious indifference. When the preacher arrived the old man was sitting on the front porch reading the Bible. Truly shocked, the preacher said, "I see you are reading the Bible."

Then came the real shocker: "Yes, parson, I just wanted to find out what Job did for boils."

✦ **Behind every act there is a motive.**

A census taker asked the man who came to the door, "Are you a Christian?"

"Yes, I have been for five years, but nobody in this community has ever found it out."

✦ **A tree is known by its fruit.**

A professor in a business class stated, "It acclimatizes you for business to start from scratch."

A freshman spoke up: "Especially if it's a flea market."

✦ **It takes a lot of scratching to make a business succeed.**

*O*ne cold Sunday night when the temperature was about 20 degrees, burglars broke into a church building. For obvious reasons, they didn't want to turn on any lights. So they had to stumble around in the dark. Lo and behold, one of them fell into the baptistry and splashed water everywhere. The next morning there was the evidence of the water and footprints to prove it.

At the next gathering the minister explained what happened and concluded by saying, "We got a new member Sunday night. He just didn't leave his name and address."

✦ **Darkness can destroy us rather than protect us.**

A young preacher who was prospecting for a job visited a family before preaching at the Sunday evening service. When dinner time came he was asked to dine with them. But he politely refused, saying, "I always preach better if I don't eat beforehand."

On the way back to the home of the host and hostess, he asked, "What do you think of my preaching?"

The host replied, "Young man, you might as well have *et*."

✦ **Speaking can be affected by either stomachs too full or heads too empty.**

a psychiatrist assured a mother and father: "Don't be alarmed if your son likes to make mud pies, or even if he tries to eat them—it's normal."

The mother responded: "I don't think so, and I'm sure his wife doesn't either."

✦ **What's acceptable for a child is not always acceptable for an adult.**

a farmer stated that he had learned from experience that when cholera breaks out among his hogs and one takes it and lingers on and on, it has a much better chance of getting well than one that takes it and dies at first.

✦ **You can't beat down-to-earth logic.**

a lady was very proud of her ancestry, stating that her family came over on the Mayflower. Then in her snobbish manner she asked another woman, "Does your family go back very far?"

"Yes, all the way back to the Garden of Eden; and I would prove it to you, except the Serpent ate up the records," answered the perceptive woman.

✦ **All of us have a lineage that runs back to the first couple.**

a budding entrepreneur sold milk from his cow to people in a nearby village. He figured how much money he was making. Then he figured again how much more he could make if he didn't feed her. Everything worked well until the cow dropped dead.

✦ He who wants the milk must feed the cow.

T here was a preacher who was known to be man-pleasing, soft-soaping, wishy-washy in all his sermons. It was said that he would preach on neither heaven nor hell, and all because he had friends in both places.

✦ The world will not follow the person of no conviction— not for long.

T wo golfers were playing close to the street. A funeral procession passed by and one of them pulled off his hat and stood in solemn attention.

After the procession passed, the other one said, "Bill, I want to commend you; I didn't know you had such a respectful feeling toward the dead."

In somber tones Bill replied, "Yes, if she had lived until Saturday, we would have been married 20 years."

✦ What we treasure most there our priorities will be.

a retired preacher who wanted to buy a farm went to look at one. The owner walked him over the land, including some bottom land which backed up against a little river.

The preacher, noticing some mud marks four feet high on the trees, asked, "Does this river ever overflow?"

"No, no," responded the owner.

The preacher continued, "If it doesn't overflow, what are those mud marks four feet high doing on those trees?"

Hesitatingly, the would-be seller replied, "Mud marks? What mud marks? You mean those marks on the trees? The hogs, while scratching themselves, rubbed up against the trees and left those marks."

When they got back to the house the owner inquired, "Well, parson, do you think you would like to buy this farm?"

The discerning preacher replied, "No, I guess not. But I tell you what—I would like to get a start of those hogs."

✦ **Exercise your senses to discern both truth and falsehood.**

*W*hile a preacher was visiting a family, the father—wanting to make a good impression—told his little son, "Go get the good old book we love so dearly in this family."

Two minutes later the little fellow came back with the Sears catalog.

✦ **Be cautious of trying to make an undeserved impression.**

a s two children were playing, one threatened the other by saying, "If you don't do right, the devil will get you."

"No," said the other, "there ain't no devil. He's just your daddy, like Santa Claus."

+ **If you act like the devil, you may be mistaken as the devil.**

a church member complained to the preacher about such high pay for only one hour of work on Sunday morning.

The preacher explained, "This reminds me of the farmer who took a load of wheat to the elevator. The cashier also grumbled, 'A lot of pay for such little work.' 'That wasn't all the work,' replied the farmer, 'I was just unloading.' Now that describes my preaching; it isn't all the work I do—I'm just unloading."

+ **There can be more work than what meets the eye or the ear.**

a braham Lincoln told about a man who was tarred and feathered and ridden out of town on a rail who stated, "I don't think I would have liked it, except for the honor of it."

+ **There can be honor in being persecuted.**

a businessman who had just gotten a big government contract was asked to speak to a civic club. Though he had a week to think about it, he still wasn't sure of what to discuss. Just as he was ready to walk into the banquet hall he saw on the door PUSH. He said to himself, "That's it! An essential ingredient of success."

In his speech he said, "I want to discuss one of the most vital necessities of success. If you will turn and look on the door, you will see what it is." They turned and looked and saw the word PULL.

✦ Pull helps but there is no substitute for push.

o n Monday morning a worker said to a fellow worker, "What did your preacher preach on yesterday?"

"Sin."

The inquirer continued, "What about it?"

"I couldn't tell for sure, but I thought maybe he might be against it," was the befuddled reply.

✦ The world demands forthrightness.

*M*any years ago a young medical doctor would make calls with an older doctor for about three years before he went out on his own. He could tend their horses, observe the experienced doctor's diagnosis and the remedy prescribed. The young doctor had a beautiful black horse that the older doctor had tried and tried to acquire, but to no avail.

During the last week of their work together the older doctor said, "Son, I've taught you everything I know about health and medicine; however, there's one thing I haven't taught you that will make you more money than everything else combined."

"Doc, tell me," implored the young man.

"No, I won't tell you unless you give me that black horse."

"You won't?"

"No, no."

"All right," responded the young doctor, "the horse is yours. What is it?"

"Keep them in bed," was the terse reply.

"But, doctor," inquired the young man, "suppose they want to know what is wrong with them?"

The old man said, "Just tell them they have black horse fever."

✦ **Ulterior motives can help one at the expense of others.**

a man walking on a country road waved down a motorist and inquired, "Have you seen a group of people up the road?" On learning that he had, the inquirer continued, "I had better hurry on up there—I'm their leader."

They had already gone off and left their leader.

✦ **A leader must lead or eventually be left behind.**

I n a wedding ceremony the preacher asked the nervous, trembly groom: "Do you take this woman to be your lawfully wedded wife, to have and to hold, for better or worse, for richer or poorer, in health or sickness..."

At this point the bride exclaimed, "Papa, stop that preacher; he'll talk him out of it."

✦ **Marriage is a bold commitment, evidently bigger than many couples realize.**

a young man who had gotten his degree in architecture and construction went back to his home on the farm. The father, believing he had a real expert, put the boy to building a smokehouse. The young specialist who had brought his education back home in the trunk of his car made a big hole in the wall for their big cat and a little hole for their little cat.

The father tactfully explained, "Son, don't you know that both the big cat and the little cat can go through the same big hole?"

The boy knew he had to get out of this idiocy somehow, so after thinking a few moments he said, "Dad, when I slam my foot down and yell 'scat,' I mean 'scat'"!

✦ **Planning ahead can save us from puny explanations later.**

a teacher and her children were eating their lunch. While the teacher was eating an apple, she gulped, turned faintly pale and said, "Oh, I've just eaten a worm."

"That's not so bad, think of the poor worm," consoled Tommy.

✦ **Things can always be worse.**

L ittle Ruth was permitted to sit in her mother's place at the dinner table one evening when the mother was away from home.

Her brother, just a little older and disliking the arrangement, said, "Now you're the mother tonight. How much is three times eight?"

Ruth kindly replied, "I'm busy. Ask your father."

✦ **Children learn from their parents.**

a lady was still laughing when she went back to work Monday morning. She stated that she was sitting next to another lady in church Sunday, and it was soon evident that the preacher was going to clean house. After about 15 minutes she whispered to the other lady, "It sure looks like the preacher is going to straighten Hazel out."

"If he straightens Hazel out, he's sure going to be one tired man," quipped the other lady.

✦ **Some jobs call for more than human effort.**

P erhaps the most famous of all epitaphs reads:

"Stranger, stop as you pass by,

As you are now, so once was I.

As I am now, you soon will be,

And so prepare to follow me."

Someone who evidently gave it some consideration wisely added these two lines:

"To follow you I'm not content

Until I know which way you went."

✦ **If the blind leads the blind, both will fall into the ditch—or worse.**

*a*t a social gathering a woman said, "Doctor, can you tell me who that horrible looking man is over there?"

"I can," replied the doctor, "that is my brother."

There was an awkward pause while the woman racked her brain for something to say. The doctor was enjoying her discomfort. She then stammered, "Oh, I beg your pardon. How silly of me not to have seen the resemblance."

✦ **An effort to correct a blunder can sometimes make it worse.**

*a*man received a letter from an out-of-town attorney. Not understanding it, he went to his own local lawyer with it, who said, "Go ahead and read it to me." This is it: "Your Uncle James, having come to advanced years, having suffered financial reverses, being debilitated by the encroachment of senility, in a moment of temporary dementia, perpetrated his own demise."

The lawyer said, "You want to know what it means? Well, it means this: Your Uncle James grew old, lost his wad, went nuts, and bumped himself off."

✦ **It is better to speak five words with the understanding than ten thousand words in an unknown tongue.**

a man who had a job grading oranges according to size finally quit. When asked why, he answered, "Those decisions were killing me."

✦ **Life calls for one decision after another; and when one cannot decide, action is paralyzed.**

After World War II there was a cruise ship sailing off the coast of England. On board was a magician who entertained the passengers. Also, there was a parrot in on the act. Each time the sleight-of-hand man performed some astounding feat, the parrot squawked, "Faker, faker," and the audience roared. One day just as the magician waved his handkerchief and mumbled some hocus-pocus, the ship hit a mine and blew up.

The next morning at daylight there was the magician sitting on one end of a raft and the parrot on the other end. After a pause, the parrot said, "Okay, smarty, you win; but what did you do with the ship?"

✦ A faker may appear to win when he doesn't.

a young man in preaching his first sermon was scared half to death, but he continued with a trembly voice and shaky knees.

At the back one man yelled, "Louder! Louder! We can't hear!"

A man at the front stood up and said, "I can and I shall be glad to swap places with you."

✦ **In a world of crackpot ideas, what we don't hear may be better than what we do hear.**

a woman had the nerve-wracking problem of living with a husband who got drunk every Saturday night. She talked, she prayed, she kept talking—talked so much that he began to look upon her as a devilish nag. Finally, thinking she might scare him to his senses, she dressed up like Satan, pitchfork and all, and stationed herself in the lane going to their house about a mile from the little town. As he wobbled down that lane one Saturday night, she stepped out and said, "I'm the devil."

He hiccuped two or three times, stuck out his hand and said, "Shake, Old Boy. I married your sister."

✦ **Never go so far in trying to help another that it's interpreted as nagging.**

One Sunday evening a preacher blasted Satan in his sermon, worked him over plainly and pointedly.

Some young men decided to have some fun. They hid behind a hedge; and as the preacher was walking home, one of them—dressed up like Satan—stepped out and said, "I heard all the bad things you said about me tonight."

The preacher in a trembly voice replied, "Hold on. Wait a moment. You know I've been your friend all along."

✦ **Profession and actuality are not always the same.**

Many years ago sermons were so long that it was sort of a contest between the preacher and the audience to see which could last the longest.

A child less than two years old was sitting with his parents at the front. After the preacher had preached and preached and preached, the little boy stood up on the pew, looked back over the audience and said, "I think it's about time to have some beans." Those grim-faced members went into convulsions and the poor preacher was never able to get it back together again.

✦ **Short sermons may be more effective and relevant.**

*T*he principal of a school opened his mail one day and there was a single sheet of paper with only one word on it: "FOOL."

At the next assembly he stated, "I get letters from people who forget to sign their names; but yesterday I received a letter from someone who signed his name but forgot to write the letter."

✦ **An anonymous letter is an unfair way to fight a battle—lets one make a strike without being hit back.**

a preacher stated in his speech at a preacher's luncheon that he dreamed he went to heaven and looked around and James Watts, a fellow preacher, wasn't there. This produced a few giggles.

Then it was time for Watts to reply. He said, "You know, that's funny, Jim. I also had a dream last night. I dreamed I went to heaven and the Lord gave me a piece of chalk and said, 'Go over there and write down all your sins.' And just at that time I met you leaving. I said, 'Jim, what are you doing? Why are you going that way?' And you said, 'I'm going to get some more chalk.'" And they roared.

✦ **When it comes to writing down our sins let's hope we don't run out of chalk.**

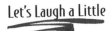

at an evening political rally held in the park the bugs were everywhere, attracted by the bright lights. Each time the speaker inhaled he ran the risk of sucking in one of them. Finally, he did. His audience reacted with alarm and wonder: What will he do? After a little gasping and coughing he said, "That bug got what was coming to him. He should have watched where he was going."

✦ **Maintaining poise in a crisis is a big plus in life.**

a soldier in the Civil War who wanted to play it safely put on the coat of a Northern soldier—a blue coat— and the pants of a Southern soldier—gray pants—and tiptoed onto the battlefield. He got shot by both sides.

✦ **The issues of life call for us to be on one side or the other.**

some people were watching the hounds chase a rabbit. They shouted, "Run rabbit! Run! Run!"

"I appreciate your words of encouragement," declared the rabbit, "but why doesn't somebody call off the hounds?"

✦ **We need to back up our talk with our deeds.**

t was the custom of Granny, who was nearly blind, to visit every newborn baby in the village. She was known to always say exactly the same thing about every baby.

Seeing Granny coming down the road, two mischievous boys removed the baby to a back room, put the lazy tomcat in the baby's crib and pulled the blanket up over him. In came Granny, who pulled back the cover and said, "I'll say one thing; he's the exact image of his daddy."

✦ **The same words don't fit all occasions.**

boy who was all banged up went into a boy scout meeting. The scoutmaster looked at him and inquired, "What happened to you?"

He replied, "I was helping an old lady across the street."

"But why did you get hurt?"

"She didn't want to go," answered the boy.

✦ **It is hard to help people who don't want to be helped.**

a preacher went home with a farm family for dinner. The good wife served the customary preacher dinner: chicken, two young roosters. The preacher lived up to his reputation and ate a large portion.

After the meal the father and the preacher went to the back yard to stretch a little. An old rooster jumped up on the fence and began to crow. Whereupon, the preacher remarked: "You know, that rooster is crowing like he has something to be proud of."

The old man replied, "He does. Two of his sons just entered the ministry."

✦ **The most unaccomplished can find something for which to be proud.**

I n a business meeting of a church—held while the preacher was out of town—they got into a discussion of what could be done to get the preacher to shorten his sermons.

One member suggested, "Let's install a clock."

Another one replied, "No, that won't have any effect. I am against it. But I'll tell you what I am for—let's present him a calendar."

✦ **Time is very valuable, a commodity in short supply.**

*a*s the doctor examined the baby, the mother went through the doctor's pill bag. With a sudden burst of enthusiasm, she said, "Why don't you give her these pink pills? They match her socks."

✦ **In curing our woes, pretty medicine doesn't help.**

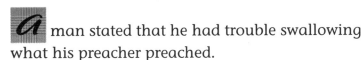

a man stated that he had trouble swallowing what his preacher preached.

"Why?"

"I can't handle it; it's too thick for a spoon and too thin for a fork," he replied.

✦ **Mush may be all right for the stomach but not very good for the soul.**

*a*t a wedding dinner, marked with joy and festivity, the crowd insisted that the groom speak. He timidly refused. Then they chanted: "Speech, groom! Speech, groom"!

Realizing they wouldn't quit until he spoke, he decided to give it a try. He nervously stood up and placed a hand on the shoulder of the bride and said, "Folks, this thing has been forced upon me."

✦ **The real test of a husband is not in the speech that's made at the wedding dinner.**

a minister who answered his telephone heard this request: "Send over to my house a case of Scotch whiskey."

The preacher recognized the voice as that of a prominent Amen member. Wanting to shock him, he said, "I am your minister."

Did the member apologize? No! He reprimanded, "Preacher, what are you doing answering the telephone at the liquor store?"

✦ **We often judge others by our own behavior.**

a fter Junior returned home from Sunday School his mother asked him what he heard.

"Just a loafing story," was Junior's reply.

"I've never heard that one. Tell me about it," replied the mother.

"Oh, somebody loafs and fishes," stated Junior.

✦ **There's a time for working and there's a time for loafing, but they don't mix well.**

T here's Henry Smith: He won't drive his car to church; neither will he ride the church bus; he's waiting for the hearse to take him.

✦ **The hearse has taken many people to church who refused to go in any other vehicle.**

*O*n Monday morning an old man went down the street at a brisk pace, tapping his cane with every step. He went into a store that was operated by a church official. He said, "Brother Brown, our new preacher is the smartest man I've ever seen—he agrees with me on everything."

✦ **Our appraisal of a person's intellect may depend on how much his views are like ours.**

a sheep rancher hired a man to herd his sheep on a ranch some 30 miles from his home in town. After about three months the herder went into town and told the rancher: "You are going to have to get me some more sheep to herd. I've run out of sheep."

✦ **Just to be on the job is not enough—each should remember why he is there.**

*a*n usher was asked to comment on the kind of people that make up the membership of the church.

Here's his insight: "They're exceedingly good, very polite, greatly gracious and extremely kind—until someone else gets in their pew."

✦ **A person can worship God in any pew but not with any heart.**

a mother in a supermarket was rolling her baby in a grocery cart. She overheard one clerk say to another, "Look at that baby; that's the ugliest baby I ever saw."

The mother became furious, bawled out the clerk and demanded to see the manager. To him she said, "I've been insulted. I've never been so mad in all my life."

The manager interrupted her, "Hold on, hold on. I'll make it right. I want to do the right thing. Just to show you I want to do the right thing, here's a banana for your little monkey."

✦ **How easy it is for one to open his mouth and stick his foot in it.**

*A*s a visitor at church listened to the preacher, he said, "That's pretty good. I'm going to give $10.00." After another 15 minutes the listener said, "No, I'm going to give only $5.00." After another 15 minutes he said, "No, I'm not going to give a cent." After a few more minutes he was saying, "So help me, I'm going to take out $5.00."

✦ **Too much talk can ruin a sale.**

A revivalist was very persuasive and insistent that people respond during the invitation hymn. Nobody budged. Then another song with the same tender pleadings. Finally, a boy arose and headed toward the front. Encouraged, the preacher said, "And a little child shall lead them." As the boy got to the front, he turned to the left, entered a hall, and went into a bathroom.

✦ **Before we follow people we need to know where they're going.**

*O*n a crowded subway a man offered his seat to a lady. She fainted. When she came to she thanked him and he fainted.

✦ **Chivalry and politeness should not be so rare that they produce fainting.**

a woman, highly frustrated, finally went to a counselor. She felt that her husband was mistreating her and she wanted advice on how to improve their relationship. The psychologist advised, "Return good for evil."

The woman replied, "Maybe that will help. There's one thing sure: hot dishwater hasn't done any good."

✦ **Returning evil for evil only compounds the problem.**

m any years ago Robert Burns, the national poet of Scotland, attended church in a strange town. He thought it was the coldest, unfriendliest church he had ever seen. Nobody spoke to him; all bypassed him as if he had the plague. As he was leaving, he dropped this little poem on a pew:

"As cauld a wind as ever blew;

A caulder kirk, and in't but few;

As cauld a minister's e'er spak;

Ye'll all be hot ere I come back."

✦ **Friendliness opens doors—and hearts; unfriendliness closes them.**

a preacher made a strong and impassioned appeal for money to build a new building to replace their crumbly one.

A rich man stood and said that he would give $5,000.00. But immediately a piece of plaster fell from the ceiling, hit him on the shoulder, and he said, "I will go up to $10,000,00."

After he sat down, some more plaster struck him, and he shouted, "Preacher, I will give $20,000.00!"

He sat down and a larger chunk hit him on the head, and he exclaimed, "Preacher, I will give $40,000.00!"

Then a deacon got in the act. He shouted, "Lord, hit him again! Hit him again"!

✦ **It shouldn't take falling plaster to knock some sense of priorities into our head.**

a young man in college, having run out of money, sent this telegram to his father:

"No mon, no fun, your son."

In reply, he received this telegram from his father:

"Too bad, how sad, your dad."

✦ **Money isn't everything, but it is a convenience when one is hungry.**

a West Texas cowboy had an itch that was driving him into frantic behavior. Finally, after no relief, he ran and jumped into a cactus plant. His classic explanation was: "Well, at the time it seemed like it was the thing to do."

✦ **Some solutions can be worse than the problem.**

*T*wo cowboys riding the range came across two buffaloes. One cowboy commented: "Look at those unsightly beasts; I think they are the ugliest creatures I ever saw in my life."

As they rode away, one buffalo commented: "I think I just heard a discouraging word."

✦ **Thoughtless words can be so cruel.**

*a*t a church business meeting they were in the process of selecting a chairman. Nominations were in order.

One observant member suggested the name of a retired man who had recently moved into their community. He gave this supporting statement: "I feel sure he's well qualified, because he's been the foreman of a circus."

✦ **We should always remember whether we are running a church or a circus.**

a man cut a puppy's tail off one inch at a time. When asked why he did it inch by inch, he said, "So it wouldn't hurt so much."

✦ **Hard drastic action sometimes is less cruel than merciful piecemeal actions.**

a mother told the school teacher that her six-year-old boy was very mischievous, but that it was inadvisable to punish him because he was so sensitive. She continued, "I'll tell you what you can do. If he does anything wrong, don't say anything to him—just slap the kid next to him and that will scare him to do better."

✦ **Unfair and inconsiderate people make life hard for others.**

I n a village church they were discussing the possibility of putting in a chandelier. Some were for it. Some were against it. But it was Uncle Bill who brought down the house. Without mincing words, he stated: "Before we go any further we need to do some thinking. First, who's going to play it. And, in the second place, what does it sound like?"

✦ **Before we are against something, we should find out about it.**

Years ago a Texas farmer who had suddenly become rich out of oil rushed into an airport to buy a ticket.

The clerk asked, "Where to, mister?"

He replied, "Anyplace. It doesn't matter. I'm just in a big hurry to get going."

✦ **Direction is more important than speed.**

As the funeral procession stopped in the street not far from the burial site, the preacher's wife walked ahead, got too close to the grave, slipped and fell in. As she emerged, a drunk who was lying behind a bush rallied, looked, squinted and said, "If it ain't the ressurrection morning, and Sarah is the first one out of the grave."

✦ **We don't always see what we think we see.**

A new minister was nervous as he arose to speak at a prestigious banquet—but he was honest.

He began: "Before I arrived tonight, there were two who had a little knowledge of what I was going to say, the Lord and I. Now only the Lord knows."

✦ **Sometimes our train of thought just can't get started.**

a frontiersman was asked why he rode the horse and his wife walked by his side. He candidly replied, "She got no horse."

✦ **Self-centeredness can block compassion toward others.**

*W*hile a preacher was visiting a family in a rural area, he—known for his compromising preaching—sat with the husband on the front porch. They sat facing a little two-lane highway with a line running down the middle. The preacher observed the chickens crossing the highway, but one hen stopped and sat down in the middle. This prompted him to say, "Look at that hen. Why did she stop in the middle?"

"Because she wants to lay it on the line," answered the old man, hoping the preacher would get the point.

✦ **People in public life should be forthright—lay it on the line.**

A person who was given a dictionary as a birthday gift later commented: "It's an excellent book and I appreciate it, but I don't find it very interesting because it changes subjects so often."

✦ **Of making many books there is no end, but the best ones fill a helpful purpose.**

A man fell out of a 40-story building. All the way down he yelled, "Everything's all right so far."

✦ **The time comes in a person's life when optimism must give way to realism.**

*a*lfred said, "My speech went over big. After I finished they kept yelling, 'Fine! Fine'"!

"Yeah, if you'd talked ten more minutes, they'd been yelling, 'Put him in jail.'"

✦ **There is an inclination to interpret words in keeping with our wishes.**

*T*here was an elderly preacher who often would go before a congregation and begin as follows: "Before I start talking, I want to say something."

✦ **A person can talk and not say anything.**

a new employee came in late for work the first four days of the week. Then on the fifth day the upset foreman said, "Wait a moment, don't you know what time we start to work here?"

"No, sir," said the employee, "everybody is always working when I get here."

✦ **Some explanations make matters worse.**

There is the story of an ox and a donkey that worked together as a team, pulling the wagon and the plow. But the ox started playing sick to keep from working. He found it more enjoyable to lie around in the stall and eat hay. This put a double burden on the poor donkey.

One day when the ox pretended to be sick, the donkey had to pull the wagon to town and back all by himself. After the donkey got back home, the ox asked, "How did you make out?"

"Not very good," replied the donkey, "I got awfully tired."

"Did the old man say anything about me?" queried the ox.

"No," replied the donkey, "but he did have a long talk with the butcher."

✦ **No one can shirk his duty forever and get by with it.**

*a*s the contribution plate was being passed at church a little boy noticed that a richly dressed woman beside him was making no effort to get any money to give. Just before the basket was ready to pass her, he handed her a nickel and said, "Here, lady, put my nickel in and I'll crawl under the bench."

✦ **A child may have a conscience stronger than some older people.**

a father and his little boy went out walking. The little fellow had to take three steps to his father's one. After a while the father said, "Son, am I walking too fast?"

"No, but I am," replied the boy.

✦ **Let us be aware of the other person's difficulties.**

*T*o enhance the choir, the minister's wife sang in it. One Sunday as they sat in service, a father whispered to his nine-year-old girl: "Do you know the minister's wife?"

"Oh, yes," was the answer, "she's one of the chorus girls."

✦ **Out of the mouth of babes—look out.**

a woman who was beginning to get sensitive about her age applied for a job.

As the interviewer looked over the sheet she had filled in, he said, "I see your birthday is September 12. Which year, please?"

"Every year," replied the applicant.

✦ **A quick lip can come in handy.**

w e do have prayer in government facilities. The U.S. Senate, which has a chaplain to pray, is an example. However, it was Will Rogers, the great humorist, who said, "The chaplain in the Senate doesn't pray for the senators—he just takes one look at the senators and prays for the country."

✦ **All, whether kings or peasants, are so imperfect as to be in need of prayer.**

A minister who was seeking to move to another church was asked why he was leaving his present pulpit.

He replied: "Sickness and loneliness. They're all sick of me, and I'm tired of standing alone."

✦ **There's nothing like telling it like it is.**

*W*hile a young man was away in college he wrote his family back home: "One of my professors is a parrot."

A few days later he got a letter from his mother which stated: "Son, we didn't quite understand what you meant when you said that one of your professors is a parrot. Talked to the preacher about it and he said, 'I don't know. Beats me. when I was in college all of my professors were people, but that was a long time ago and maybe they have made a lot of improvement since then.'"

✦ **Be discerning; never squawk just anything you hear.**

a man who was always having to chase the wolf away from his door explained why it's so hard for him to have any money. He said, "The reason is: our neighbors are always buying something we can't afford."

✦ **Let the neighbors go to the poorhouse by themselves.**

T here is so much opposition to prayer in the public schools that if a student is caught down on his knees, he had better hope he's gambling instead of praying.

✦ **When gambling is looked upon with more favor than praying, it is time to do some soul-searching.**

W hen a college student was asked to define "medieval," he wrote, "partly bad."

✦ **Education is where you find it—not just in college.**

a student in college received this information in a letter from his mother: "Your rich old uncle Ned is very sick. I called the hospital about an hour ago and asked about him. The lady said he is awfully, awfully sick—in fact, there are three college presidents in the room with him right now."

✦ **Oh, the gravitational pull of money!**

*a*t a church service the minister, while waxing eloquently on optimism, went so far as to say, "An optimist is one who will eat hash in the dark."

An old man spoke out a little louder than he intended: "And a pessimist is one who has." It nearly broke up the service.

✦ **Our perspectives are influenced by our experiences.**

*W*e have observed that some parents have trouble naming a new baby. Others don't—they have rich relatives.

✦**Money talks—and money names babies.**

a man in his mid-years complained that nature has played a trick on us. He stated, "Why couldn't nature have heaped all of life's problems on us at 16 when we knew everything."

✦ **Time teaches us that we don't have all the answers.**

*I*n an effort to stop people from praying to be heard of men, the Good Book says something about going into the closet, shutting the door, and praying to God in secret. However, this is a hard command for some people to obey, because their closet is so filled with skeletons.

✦ **Skeletons in the closet don't have to speak—there are enough gossipers that will speak for them.**

A frowny man with a face so long that he could eat corn out of the bottom of a churn asked a humorist who had just told a joke, "Do you think God goes for jokes?"

"Yes, I know he does," replied the comic, "because He created you."

✦ **Let Solomon's remedy have its place: "A merry heart doeth good like a medicine."**

*I*f they don't have telephones in heaven, some people would be awfully unhappy if they went there.

✦ **How miserable some people would make heaven if it were furnished with telephones.**

*M*oney talks. Its favorite message is "Goodbye."

✦ **While thrift is commendable, don't squeeze your money so tightly that it can't say anything good.**

a high school senior was given a car by his parents. Being in ecstasy, he stopped at a garage and asked a mechanic, "How can you tell how much horsepower this car has?"

"Just raise the hood and count the plugs," was the reply.

The young man had another question: "How much mileage should I get?"

"Per gallon or per finder?" replied the mechanic.

✦ **It's one thing to own a car, but it's something else to have the responsibility of driving it.**

a little boy asked his daddy to teach him to shave.

"Why?" inquired the father.

"Because my teacher said that the men who get to heaven will get there only by a close shave."

His sister interrupted: "Could this be why the pictures of angels never show any with whiskers?"

✦ **One of the attractions of heaven to some men is—the new bodies won't require shaving.**

a patient went to see a psychologist concerning his depression.

The doctor stated: "Don't look for the negative; try to see the positive."

"I've just had a cancer test," replied the patient, "and I've been hoping for a negative report."

✦ **Life consists of its positives and negatives, and there's a place and time for each.**

a college appointed two local preachers as chaplains of the football team.

The all-out fans wouldn't dare think of this as politics. They gave it an interpretation of specialty: an offensive chaplain and a defensive chaplain.

✦ **There are more ticks in politics than in an eight-day clock.**

y ears ago a preacher in a revival was staying in a home that had bed bugs. (It was the age of no pesticides—just pests.) One night after the preacher had suffered bite after bite he got up, lighted a lamp, and caught one of them. He pinned it on the wall along with a note which read: "He died that I might live."

✦ **Vicariousness lets us live.**

One fussy child said to another, "You wearing those old shoes and your daddy is a shoe cobbler."

The other one replied, "That ain't nothing. Your daddy is a dentist, ain't he? And your little baby brother ain't got but one tooth."

✦ **Good deeds should begin at home.**

a person stated, "I was told to wait, that all things come to him that waits. And I waited. And all I got were the leftovers from the guys who got there first."

✦ **We can't win the race unless we enter it.**

*a*n alcoholic wandered from the street into a church service. At the close of the service he asked for membership, stating, "I belong with you people. One of you prayed, 'We often do things we should not do and leave undone things we should do,' and that describes me exactly."

✦ **Maybe we all have more in common than we think.**

a woman speaker before a group of women was accused of extremism.

She replied, "Oh, you don't like extremism? On the behalf of extremism let me ask you a question: Had you rather for your husband to be moderately faithful or extremely faithful?"

Silence prevailed. She had just made a lot of converts to extremism.

✦ **All of us are extremists—just in different areas.**

ears ago it became a customary pattern of dress for a woman to wear her hair in a little knot on the top of her head. But a preacher in a church disliked it, and Sunday after Sunday it became more annoying to him.

Finally, the preacher addressed the issue in the pulpit on Sunday morning. He said, "My sermon pertains to a woman's hairdo. The text is Matthew 24:17—now get it, which says, 'Top knot come down.'" But that Scripture actually reads, "Let him which is on the housetop not come down."

✦ **By perverting Scripture one can prove anything, which is no proof at all.**

n engineer was asked how it's possible for the tongue to make 1100 revolutions a minute.

He replied, "It can't unless the brain is in neutral."

✦ **It's unfortunate when the tongue gets disconnected from the brain.**

ne reason the Ten Commandments are so brief and understandable is that the Author was not trying to impress anybody with His notable scholarship and linguistic ability.

✦ **Simplicity has more fans than complexity.**

*M*arriage can defy arithmetic. It is said of wedlock: "Two are better than one." This is assuming that each is worth something; otherwise, one is better than two.

✦ **Numbers don't always give strength, and this is true of some marriages.**

a man complained of being awfully ill. His wife called the medical doctor, who came as quickly as he could.

The doctor asked him, "Do you have any pain in your chest?" The patient replied, "You're the doctor."

Then the doctor inquired, "Do you have any pain in your throat?" The patient said, "You're the doctor."

The the doctor asked, "Do you have any pain in your abdomen?" Again the man on the bed replied, "You're the doctor."

The doctor turned to the man's wife and said, "I can't do him any good. Call Dr. Cardova."

Aghast, she said, "Doctor, isn't Dr. Cardova a horse doctor?"

He replied, "Yes, but only a horse doctor can do that donkey any good."

✦ **Sometimes a patient needs a jolt.**

*I*n a family where the woman constantly complained of being too hot, the husband suggested to her that—in the event of her death—she could best be remembered by using one of her most frequent statements as an epitaph on her tombstone: "Turn down the thermostat, I'm getting too hot!"

✦ **The appropriateness of a statement is dependent on the circumstances.**

A horseman stated that he had a horse seventeen feet tall.

"You mean seventeen hands tall, don't you?" replied the other man.

"What did I say?" inquired the owner.

"You said seventeen feet tall," replied the listener.

"Well, if I said that horse is seventeen feet tall, that horse is seventeen feet tall," was the emphatic statement.

✦ **Some people need to pray, "Lord, help me to be always right, for I'm too stubborn to ever change when I'm wrong."**

father and his youngster were touring the zoo. It was outside the lion's cage that the father got his shocker.

The little girl asked, "Daddy, if a lion gets out and eats you up, what bus do I take to get home?"

✦ **Just thinking of self is something we should all outgrow.**

When the preacher walked through the door, his disturbed wife demanded, "Where have you been the last three hours? Dinner is cold."

"I met Mrs. Smith downtown, asked her how she's feeling and she told me," sighed the weary minister.

✦ **Experience teaches us not to ask some people about their ailments.**

At a political rally a speaker was running long over time. Finally, in disgust, the master of ceremonies raised his gavel and as he came down swiftly the end of it came off and hit a man in the first row. The man slumped and moaned, "Hit him again, he's still talking."

✦ **A basic principle of effective speaking is to shut up when you're through.**

A minister said, "The Bible speaks of fishermen and fish. Right now, I wish I were a fish. Ever since a can of worms was opened in this church, they have been wiggling and crawling everywhere; and where they may go, only God knows."

✦ **Never open a can of worms unless you have a big bucket, for they will multiply.**

*T*here are three very effective kinds of communication: telephone, telegraph, tell-a-gossip.

✦ **Gossip is the fastest communication that leaves nothing unsaid.**

*S*peaking of jokes, Adam had one thing in his favor: When he told a joke to his wife, he didn't have to hear her say, "I've heard that one before."

✦ **Think how many things you have heard before that are still worthwhile.**

a part of the man's prayer at church went like this: "Oh Lord, use me in thy work, especially in an advisory capacity."

✦ **While we need advisers, somebody has to work—tote the wood and carry the water.**

*I*t's easy to spot a pessimist on vacation. He will never look at the ocean twice for fear that if he looks the second time he will see that it has dried up.

✦ **Our world is an optimistic one. The sun keeps shining, the earth keeps turning, day and night succeed each other, and the seasons come and go.**

a man was being interviewed for a teaching position in a small-town school. A trustee said, "Would you say that a hen lays or lies?"

Not knowing, he replied, "I don't care whether she lays or lies, provided that when she cackles she's not lying."

Thinking that was cute, they hired him.

✦ **In the race of life, the fast thinker comes in ahead.**

I n commending the work of the outreach minister the pulpit minister stated, "In his tireless work he visits many homes, and you may rest assured they're all happy when he leaves."

✦ **Do we generate happiness in visiting or does it come because of our departure?**

S ome members of a church were discussing their new minister who had just finished theological school.

"He acts like he thinks he's God," stated one person.

But the one who took the blue ribbon said, "I wouldn't be a bit surprised if he starts autographing Bibles."

✦ **Schools educate brains, but they don't hand them out.**

he next day after the wedding the groom's little brother commented, "I'm afraid Sam's in trouble."

"Why do you say that?" asked the mother.

"I was suspicious of it all during the wedding when I noticed that the bride's family was so happy; and then I was sure of it when I heard her little sister say, "Boy, are we glad to get this thing off our hands."

✦ **Words can be so misunderstood.**

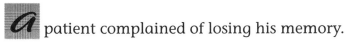

a patient complained of losing his memory.

The doctor assured him: "If you're losing your memory, don't worry about it. In your state, you're apt to soon forget it."

✦ **Memory is one of the finest attributes—especially if it can turn off the unpleasant.**

*D*uring the Civil War Granny looked out the window and saw the Union soldiers coming. She grabbed a broom and ran to meet them.

One of her sons yelled, "Granny, Granny, come back here. What do you think you can do?"

As she ran, she hollered back, "Well, at least I can let them know whose side I'm on."

✦ **The world would be better if each would stand up and be counted.**